Remember Who
Loves
You

Inspire Love

GEORGE BRADLEY

BALBOA.PRESS
A DIVISION OF HAY HOUSE

Balboa Press books may be ordered through booksellers or by contacting:

Balboa Press
A Division of Hay House
1663 Liberty Drive
Bloomington, IN 47403
www.balboapress.com
844-682-1282

Because of the dynamic nature of the Internet, any web addresses or links contained in this book may have changed since publication and may no longer be valid. The views expressed in this work are solely those of the author and do not necessarily reflect the views of the publisher, and the publisher hereby disclaims any responsibility for them.

The author of this book does not dispense medical advice or prescribe the use of any technique as a form of treatment for physical, emotional, or medical problems without the advice of a physician, either directly or indirectly. The intent of the author is only to offer information of a general nature to help you in your quest for emotional and spiritual well-being. In the event you use any of the information in this book for yourself, which is your constitutional right, the author and the publisher assume no responsibility for your actions.

Any people depicted in stock imagery provided by Thinkstock are models, and such images are being used for illustrative purposes only. Certain stock imagery © Thinkstock.

Print information available on the last page.

ISBN: 978-1-5043-7426-2 (sc)
ISBN: 978-1-5043-7427-9 (hc)
ISBN: 978-1-5043-7455-2 (e)

Library of Congress Control Number: 2017901660

Balboa Press rev. date: 11/19/2020

Now is the time
to let your true self shine and
find your voice with love.
You will amaze yourself
with how much more love you hold.
The world waits for
this kingdom of love.

Credit

I would like to give credit to the origin of the title for this book. I was a teacher for high school students that were at risk of not graduating. They shared a lot of their emotionally charged situations in their lives with us. I wanted to tell them that I loved them many times and did not. One day out of the blue as everyone was leaving I just yelled out, "Remember who loves you," and that became our official closing salutation. Students bantered over their turn to extend that farewell for the day. As I look back, I see this as the most significant contribution I made during my career as a teacher. You never know what your words of love are going to mean to someone else. Actions of love take on so much more significance when the words of love are also present.

Find Your Words of Love

These words of love have led to many awakenings for me along my path of discovery. Your path of love can take on any shape you want and you will never find its end. Love is not only part of your life's journey; love is the point of the journey. Love is about the rainbow that comes with the rain. The pot of gold will be consumed but the rainbow will always inspire. Love is a feast that will never know an empty table. Love is an appetite and not a hunger. Stay the course of love and you will find your heavenly delights. Know love for yourself and loving relationships will find you. There is a quote for every day and many affirmations to inspire and help you keep your flow of love strong. A quote a day with an affirmation to ponder will bring you many pleasures and gifts.

These quotes are not meant for publication but they are meant to be shared. Insert some of them in your wedding vows or holiday greetings and email a love message to friends and family. You will also find these quotes on posters at various social media sites for your sharing ease. Messages of love are spoken all over the world. Go to the web site: **withlovebygbradley.com** to share a quote of your creation or a personal favorite that you would like to share as a post for all to see. Perhaps, we will receive enough quotes to create another "Remember Who Loves You" book with the proceeds going world charities.

1

I can feel my heart opening in trust and faith,
Thanks to the tender warmth of your love.

2

Our love is a step upon a Golden Path of Discovery.
We are two flowers opening up to the morning sun.

3

Our meetings are full of playful and adventurous delights.
We have found each-other's child.

4

Our bodies say we are seniors but our spirit is skipping along.
We are upon a youthful adventure into the realms of love.
The free spirit of our love is secured by its ageless nature.

5

This love flows as naturally as the sweet spring sap.
The simple pleasures are part of our day.

6

I wish only to experience you as you present yourself,
Realizing that you feel the same,
Hand in hand and heart to heart.

7

There is nothing like a rainy day to contemplate,
The deepest sense of our love and contentment.

8

Why do you say all the right things?
Why do I feel so good?
It is not that I actually need to know why;
It is just my chance to say thank you!

9

There is no distance between us.
Our love is near and dear.

10

I have felt your tender touch,
And you mine.
I know we are healed in some way.

11

It is such a gift of compassion,
That you allow me to express what I feel.
So often we are feeling the same thing.

12

When I express my words of love,
I feel that I am speaking for both of us.

13

When we are apart there is both emptiness and a peace.
Apart or together, I know you feel the same.

14

It is only time that separates us when we are apart.

15

There is a humble gratitude to our love,
That knows no form of emptiness.
There is nothing for the other to fulfill.

16

Love is the seed of every flower in your garden.
Your flowers calm my mind and delight all of my senses.

17

Some will say love is fate.
Some will say it is luck.
Some will say love must be worked at.
We will say: "Our love just is."

18

Your love is a beautiful flower waiting for a table.
You are my bouquet.
I am your table.

19

I fill the wood box in anticipation of a fire that will warm
our hands,
Knowing that the spirit of our own fire is already burning.

20

We are caught in the flow of each other's love.
We drift beyond our past with love.

21

This love goes forward with its own grace.
It is a gentle breeze on a warm day.
This love is the ripple that gives the lake's surface character.

22

By some grace, our love is so.
We ride the waves knowing the comforts our love holds.
Our love progresses with the ease of a feather floating to the ground.

23

We have come upon a maturity,
That makes it possible for us to find the words,
To express our openness to each other's love.
Today is the moment we get to share our love!

24

We awaken to the dawn of this day's love.
When we talk there is joy, laughter and peace in our hearts.
When we love, there is no need for anything else.
Have I said, "Thank you for this day with you"?

25

You set the spirit of love in me free.
Today is the right time,
For matters of these hearts.

26

We felt an electrifying spark the first time we met.
The kingdom of love will be with us on our last journey together.

27

We are right for each other,
Without needing to know how it is so.

28

The nature of our Love states that,
There is so much more to come.

29

Love!
There is so much to discover.
There is more contentment than I would have guessed.

30

Words are not enough to explain this love.
We know a love that is a bridge between majesty and reality.

31

There is a feeling in its infancy,
Wishing to know more about our love.
We will be content while we grow together.

32

We express so many feelings as we get to know each other.
May we explore the depth of our heart and soul,
While the feelings of our restless spirit find their peace.

33

It does not appear that a rational mind,
Can fully interpret the marvels of our love.

34

Your love stands before me, magnificent and true.
There is no need to wonder why or what it will be.

35

Our love at all times must be free to ride on our wings.

36

Our love will always be,
Now that we took time to see.

37

Our love is as delicate as a silk thread, with the strength of
a steel rope.

38

We are constantly learning about love.
We have learned how to accept and appreciate.
We are each other's teacher.

39

This love you introduced me to feels so familiar.
I know you from somewhere.
We are reunited.

40

We surrender our hold,
So that we may find our wings,
To soar upon the wind currents of love.

41

Love is all around,
A kiss in the kitchen,
Glances as you walk by,
Side by side under a blanket,
The words, "I am home"
A laugh, a cheer, a tear,
We are, as love is.

42

Our parent's kitchen of love warmed the whole house.
The pantry was full.
The table was set.
There are many more family recipes to sample

43

We mix the ingredients for a freshly baked pie with love,
Love is so clear I can smell and taste what is now so near.
How slow time passes while the oven bakes its feast.
Our love is nourishment to all our senses.
Love sweet love, we are your bakers.

44

We find ourselves in the kitchen of our mansion of love.
This love is not the first cake ever made or the only house
with a baker.
This love is a continuation of an old recipe passed down for
generations.

45

Help us to go with the flow, fast or slow.
We just want to know each other's love,
To see more clearly,
And appreciate more dearly.

We will float on the waters of a gentle river taking us from
our past,
We will round many bends,
With love answering every question along the way.

With yesterday being a gentle memory,
We love today, again and again.

Our time is consumed by the joy of knowing each other
and love.
Our joy and our love are recorded in our book of life.

Good night, my sweet love.
May our spirits find each other's soulful embrace as we sleep.

50

I make myself ready to receive your love.
I forgive and I heal.
I set my love free.
Your love in hand with mine
Has found its rightful place.

51

We know many joys.
We know a playful happiness.
We know the beauties of nature.
We know the rewards of accomplishment.
And we know each other's love.

52

You are the marvel of our love.
You take my love to new depths.
I look forward to our next adventure.

53

This love brings me a joy,
That is different than any human pleasure.
You create the opportunity for my love to express itself.

54

We float past every awkwardness regarding love,
Like a leaf drifting down a gentle stream.

55

Our embrace is our candle of love.
The fluid dance and warmth of love's flame warms our hearts.

56

My heart is light with joy.
I am bright and free.
I feel like I am standing on a mound of feathers,
When you approach me.

57

I see your love everywhere I look.

58

Our love is the place,
Where "Good night." meets "Good morning."

59

Your voice has become the sound of love.

60

This moment of love,
Cannot be counted by the ticks on a clock alone.

61

We are two drops in an ocean of love.

62

Love does not seem to be such a dream anymore.
Our love has become the nature of my being.

63

Love changes the question we sometimes ask in life,
From "Why?" to "Why not?"

64

I open the windows to let what is inside out.
I open the door to let our neighbor in.
I clear my mind to be open to your love.

65

Every moment with you is an adventure to my inner child.
We grow older with age and younger with our love.

66

We are made for the purpose of expanding our love.
We grow in love with no seams to burst.
I keep finding room for more of you.

67

I hope you will take my hand and jump in a puddle with me.
If we like that,
We can swim a lap or two across the pool,
Then a lake, and then and then...

68

We will make it to the ocean someday.
As we float down our river of love.

69

There are many colors of light.
Our love is the light itself.

70

Our home provides comfort and security.
Our love provides the serenity of well-being.

71

Love by its nature wants to grow and expand.
Now that we know each other's love.
Our life cannot be restricted.

72

Our wants for love continues to fade.
Our wonderments regarding love grow.
We find new roads to explore,
As places to share our love comes our way.

73

This love has its marvels and its glow.
This love knows which curtain to choose.
And what doors to close.

74

Our love shines in every experience.
We don't have to imagine,
What it might be like anymore.

75

My love for you is not about the sun or the sweet rains.
My love for you is about the rainbow that it brings.

76

My love is no longer black and white;
The greys are getting lost in our kaleidoscope of colors.

77

Would you like to start this day on a walk with me?
There are many paths to choose from.
Our love is the ground we walk on.

78

Our love is the blanket of snow,
That covers everything in sight.

79

Looking into your eyes is an adventure of love.
We are captivated by each other's gaze.
Our love has become the window to our soul.

80

I look into your eyes and I see a love that is bigger than thee.
It is that gaze of love that greets the rest of the world with me?

81

We take this love as far as we can,
Everything else in our lives wants to come with us.

82

There was a time when I wanted to wrap my arms,
Around your love and hold on tight.
Now I watch you fly as I jump out of the nest to join you.

83

Whether we are working or sitting in quiet contemplation,
Our hearts soar like an eagle on the wind currents of love.

84

Our love has its own rhythm,
That is easy to dance to.

85

When I kissed you good night,
I said you were my teacher.
When I kissed you good morning,
I said, "I have found love."

86

Each expression of our love is a part of our being.
Our new normal is,
That love is normal.

87

At one time I longed for a partner's love.
Now I simply long to know you.

88

No matter how many times we walked the moonlit beach
holding hands,
No matter how many times we look at the stars while sharing
our dreams,
No matter how many acts of charity we commit to each
other and our neighbors,
Let this not be the whole story of our love.

89

We delight in each other's passions of life.
We think we have every security in each other's love.
We believe we know the treasures of an awakened self.
Let this not be the whole story of our love.

90

It is delightful when you are there to share my excitement.
I know your love is here when you are not near.

91

May we never have all the words to express this union of love.

92

Apart or together,
We will know eternal peace.

93

We are constantly seeing each other for the first time.
That is the story of our love.
Our love is about this moment that we have together.

94

The love we found is both sacred and personal.
The love we found is a story being told.
The love we found is our song being played.

95

This love might be mysterious,
But it is not a mystery.

96

The excitement of our first meeting is still with me today.
This love feels like it will go on forever.

97

There is a touch of magic, in the reality of our love.

98

The union of our love,
Has created its own world.

99

It took so little to get used to being with you,
While it takes so much to get used to being away from you.

100

There isn't a moment that I don't feel your presence.
I feel it in my heart.
I feel it in every step I take.
Your love to me is life itself.

101

The thought of the things we will do together,
Is warm recreation for our hearts and minds,
While love is our guide.

102

Colors are bright and sounds are pure,
Knowing you are near.

103

Words of love,
Are the notes of our symphony.

104

May our words of love,
Be neither deep nor profound.
May our words of love,
Be the nature of who we are to each other.

105

I feel wonderfully helpless,
Being captivated by the wonderment of who you are.

106

It is cold and blowing outside.
I am feeling a bit restless in need to stretch my wings.
I do not use this time to think about what could be,
Or what we will do.
I can fly in spirit while I know our love to be.

107

My eyes can look at the clock every hour.
My heart is stuck in the time I found your love.

108

We sit in a cocoon of love,
While we try to look beyond the fog that surrounds us.
We will feel the love that is always there,
When the cover on our day is lifted,
The vision of our love goes beyond what is near.

109

Because of love we can know each other.
Because of love we know no limits.
There are many worlds for our love to explore.

110

I feel your hand in mine.
In that touch I feel your peace and contentment,
Your appreciation of my being,
And your sincere delights in this walk together.

111

There are times when your love trembles under my fingertips.

112

Love is the big and the small, the short and the tall,
Everything and nothing.
Love is, yesterday, today, and tomorrow.
Love is one and all.
Love is both personal and institutional.
Love is up or down, inside or out, happy or sad.
Love is how I know you.

113

There would be a sense of loss if you were not there,
Such as it is with our love.
You bring love to life in all matters of life.

114

My mind is stuck on finding new words to express my love
for you.
Any word of love is a good word.

115

Let me look at our love.
What is it that I see?
Let us have another day with each other,
To be what we will be.

116

I do not want to imagine;
A fire in the fireplace without you next to me.
Our hands not finding each other anytime we are close.
Or a garden without you sitting among the flowers.
There are many images of love.
An image without you in it is not an image of love!

117

I offer you my love,
Not how much I love,
Or how well I love;
How much and what you need as love is yours.
My love is yours to do with as you wish.

118

Our love feels as free as two chipmunks chasing each other.
Each day brings a sense of adventure and playful discovery,
Knowing your love is set upon me.

119

Our love is floating on an endless breeze.
Our love is as much a part of us as the air that we breathe.

120

Our love is so different now.
We simply let that light flow.
It is our souls that know each other.

121

There are no conditions to undo,
Just my love for you.

122

Where oh where could my beautiful love be?
Perhaps sleeping or dreaming of love and laughter.
Could it be that my love is dreaming of me?
Could it be that two tender hearts have found each other?
Could be that we have awaken from our slumber?

123

We are mere children swimming in the sunlight of love.

124

Does it matter what tomorrow brings as long as today knows
your love?

125

May every one of my senses glorify this earthly day.
By allowing these delights to be,
I have discovered your love for me.

126

So much is possible in love, and I know so little.
Whatever love will be,
May we do it together,
As one heart and two minds.

127

It seems like there is more of you today than yesterday.
We grow with the flow of our love.

128

Your hands are busy in the kitchen,
But your place is at our table.

129

While I bask in the glow of the love we share.

I am compelled to say "Thank you."

But to whom do I address that acknowledgement?

There are the wings of fate that brought us together.

There are the choices of individuality that made us ready for the other.

There are the powers of respect that hold us together.

To all that is love, "Thank you."

130

It must be love!

You keep showing up in my tomorrow.

131

I am captivated by your love;

Your hold on me is like the spell,

Cast by the dance of a burning candle.

The warmth of your light,

Is a penetrating silence,

That only knows love's truth and beauty.

132

When I am with you,
I forget any prior expectation of love I have ever had.

133

Our love is like the rock in the river.
It doesn't have to do anything but be there.
The rock gives the river character.

134

Once I discovered love,
I was able to set upon a new course,
That made it possible for our paths to cross.

135

Our love is like the bolder on the mountain;
It can be a bolder and a mountain at the same time.

136

Our love is about the joy we find in each moment we are together.
Our legacy is about the love we shared.

137

To love and be loved is our gift to one another.
To be love or exist as love is our gift to the world.

138

We cannot contain the light of our love.
Our love is the most visible on the darkest days.
Our two lights cover more territory than one.

139

There is more to this love than inspiration and comfort.
There is an infinite grace to this love.

140

We use the power of our love,
To free ourselves of any unwanted thoughts or feelings.
We are reborn in the image of this love.

141

We feel like an angel is looking over us,
While it is love that is our guide.

142

As beautiful as love is,
And what a marvel it is to behold.
You are my gift of love.

143

We celebrate your birthday this day.
We celebrate our love every day.

144

Curiosity is the seed for adventure.
Adventure becomes the path of discovery.
We have found each other because of love.

145

We look out the train window,
Watching one town after another go by.
What is behind us is losing some of its hold.
Our destination will be one of many.
We ride the rails of love fully appreciating this moment together.

146

Your grace and beauty,
May take my breath away,
While it is your love that gives me life.

147

Happy Birthday, my love!
My gift to you is to be the mirror of your love.

148

There are no false perceptions regarding this love.
Love is the clay;
We are love's sculptors.

149

You have chosen me and I you,
Like children on the playground choosing play mates.
We did not think to ask why,
We saw something and that was enough.

150

To my sister:
We were yeah tall when we first met.
We were conceived with love.
We were raised with love.
We played with love.
We went off on our own and found love.
We now travel the world sharing our love.

151

We are floating on a river of love.
Many small streams have fed into our river.
The river runs wide and deep these days.
This may be a senior's love,
But the ocean is not yet in sight.

152

There is something about the love we share,
That takes us to a place where all are one.

153

I clearly feel your love,
If there is to be such a thing as a divine moment,
I am beginning to know what that might feel like.

154

The footprints of our past have met the waves of the ocean.
The beach of love awaits our new footprint.

155

This love is a heavenly condition.
That is a key part of our earthly existence.

156

I can now comprehend a love of myself.
As our souls touched,
A loving spirit woke up in me.

157

Angels and a bright light are associated with a heaven,
Where an intense feeling of love and beauty rule.
You are my angel and the love we share is our heaven.

158

The love that we embrace today,
Is but one coin in our treasure chest.

159

Each time I hear your voice,
I feel the melody of a majestic song,
Saying that we are home.

160

Our love is the light of this new day.
Your love of me is a star in my night sky.

161

I am different somehow now that I have met you.
How do I thank something that is so natural?

162

Our union, as one love, is pure and creative.
Two in love have joined the others that light the world.
Our love is part of a kingdom that will always be.

163

Our love is my breath of life.
This love feeds every one of my senses.
This love is a spirit that cleanses my soul.

164

Good morning my beautiful friend.
It seems that this love,
Is the gift of time to know each other.

165

My love for you is yesterday's news already.

166

We honor this love by embracing this moment.

167

This love is more than the comforts it brings.
This love is more than all of its pleasures.
This love is made for the life that we live.

168

Who you are and who I am,
Does not weigh us down.
This love floats on a heavenly cloud.

169

We are different somehow because of the other.
We have wings that fly and a heart that sings.
We are living a majestic love story.

170

I find it difficult to contain my love.
I avoid any temptation that would limit our love.
I thank you for choosing to be here with me.

171

There will always be new ways to express my love.
Our love has become a source of inspiration.
One chapter leads to another.
We are a book that is being written into eternity.

172

I like what you do.

I respect what you do not do.

Appreciate all that you are.

I am so grateful that you are at my side.

If this be love, so shall it be.

That we are two trees in an enchanted forest.

173

We explore the sensual being that goes with our love.

We hear the melody of our words of love.

Our hearts unite while our mind is being entertained by love.

174

You accept me as I am.

You see my needs and wants.

You just seem to understand.

Are you within me or am I within you?

175

It is not how far our love will take us.
It is how far we will take our love.

176

The love that pours from this union fills this glass,
And the glasses of those that sit at our table.

177

Our love is about the condition of love.

178

Love is my guiding light.
Your love precedes every joy I feel.

179

May the seeds of our love bring forth a beautiful family.
May the seeds of our love nourish and shelter all that sit at
our table.
May the seeds of our love be a divine spirit that grows with us.

180

Today's love is the abundance of our tomorrows.
The eyes that see the garden we plant will also see our love.

181

The love we share energizes our lives,
Like the crystal that brings life,
To a fine tuned watch.

182

Our relationship seeks its own perfection.
Our love is already perfect.

183

Your love is not just the candle that lights the room.
Your love is the campfire that we all want to sit around.

184

Your harp strings strike a chord in my heart.
There is a symphonic grace and a pure tone to your love.

185

The days come and go.
The years run together.
A mother's love is there forever.
There is no such thing as one Mother's Day.

186

Love is the horse that pulls the cart,
That is our relationship.

187

Love is the waters that our swan song floats on.

188

Love is our bouquet of mixed flowers.
The bouquet you place on our table lifts our spirits.
Our love has its own fragrance.

189

We are caught in the levity of this love.
Our footsteps barely touch the ground.

190

Our smile says that we did it with love.

191

The contentment our love brings is constant.
"I Love you." and "I Thank you."

192

We sat among the trees and felt their love.
We said thank you.
We heard them say it back,
It is the love in you that was able to see us as we truly are!
It is us that thank you!

193

I sat on the lakeshore this morning,
And notice that the impression it presented this day,
Was like no other.
So shall it be with each day of our love.

194

Our love has set us free to be as we will be.
Love has become the way and not the end.

195

I thank you with every breath I take.
Love gives us life.
Life has given us each other.

196

The sun is warm on my face.
The waters cleanse my soul.
The earth nurtures my body.
The winds bring the spirit of love to me.
Your love is my tree of life.

197

We walk the path of love together.
I fear no evil.
You, me, and love, are all that I need.

198

We strain to get a glimpse of the bird making the beautiful
sound.
Its beauty is touching.
I can hear your love song wherever I stand.

199

Your words of love have become a part of me.

200

Today, the snow clings to the trees.
Tomorrow, the sun will glisten on yesterday's snow.
The days evolve. Images change,
But not our love.

201

The winds blow.
The snow swirls.
A drift is formed with ease.
As it is with the sands that form the dunes.
So shall it be with the design of our love.

202

Love is like the sun's rays;
It reaches the earth wherever it can find a clearing between
the trees.
Our love seeks the warmth we find in those clearings,
And rests, enjoying the peace found in the shade.

203

Our love shall feed a mighty oak with a single drop of water.

204

Large snowflakes are falling straight down.
The bushes are wrapped in a blanket of snow.
They appear to be engulfed by a silent contentment.
Like the love we share, sitting by the fireplace,
Holding hands under a blanket.

205

I found the oyster with the pearl in it,
When I found you.

206

We shall blossom together,
Opening up like two lilies,
Enjoying the day's dance on the waves of love.

207

We celebrate our wonderment of love,
Like two rivers meeting the lake they feed.

208

The awe I feel in the presence of your love,
Is like a double rainbow after a gentle rain.

209

Our love sheds its gaze,
Upon a moon lit path after a fresh snow fall.
We look forward and see an endless white expanse.
We look back and see the path we have walked together.

210

Our love is as simple as the birds that sing,
The flowers that bloom,
And the waters that sparkle in the moonlight.

211

Nature does not ask why or what this love is.
Nature only waits to see how much there can be.

212

Our world of love is a garden in continuous bloom,
With a path for all to walk through.

213

I look out the window,
Imagining the trees budding,
With the stick silhouettes of winter trees turning green,
Knowing that our love is already in continuous bloom.

214

It seems that all of our senses are more alive.
Our leaves have sprung from their buds.
This is but one spring of our life together.
We know a love that looks forward to the changing seasons.

215

Good morning, my love.
We have another day to play our love song.
We will rest this evening under our patched quilt of love.

216

Good morning, my love.
The reflection on the water welcomes the rising sun.
Your love has already been introduced to my day.

217

The mirror image on the waters before me depends on the sun.
The love we share is its own reflection.

218

Our love is a part of nature's glory.
We will bathe in the day's light,
While we rest in night's peace.

219

The leaves change colors to announce a new season.
There is only one season for our love.

220

Your love teaches me so much about nature.
Nature teaches me so much about our love.

221

A spring snow fall surprises us with its beauty one more time.
The surprises that come with your love do not lose their
beauty.

222

Our love is as limitless as a sea breeze,
And the waves that approach the beach.

223

The roof overhead shelters us with love.
Our love is a mansion onto itself.

224

One flower turned to the other and said,
"Did you notice that they too are as lovely as we?"
One snow flake turned to the other and said.
"Did you notice that they too are as lovely as we?
"I am no longer as unique as I once thought."
"I am in love."

225

When we look across the surface of the lake,
We cannot see the depth of the waters below.
The love we see in each other is just the beginning.

226

You grow your garden with love and gratitude.
You place your bouquet on our table.
You enrich our home with the presence of your love.
You are my bouquet.

227

Rain drops and a gentle breeze gracefully dance upon the lake's surface,
While the deeper waters rest content.
Such as it is with our love.

228

Our love is my day and my night.
Our love is both here and there.
Love is what we are to the other.

229

Our love is:
As relentless as an ocean breeze.
As determined as a raging river.

230

The sun sparkles on the ripples,
Like diamonds on a sea of love.
One would not be without the other.
Our love would not be if it were not for you.

231

This love will be as it is.
We have become the grace of love itself.
We grow, we flow, and we unite with love.
We are a force that can carve a canyon out of mountain.

232

I imagine how the grass and the flowers await the warmth
of the sun.
I wait no more for your love.

233

The rain washes the earth,
While the flowers and plants spring to life.
Love washes away our troubles,
While your love nurtures every fiber of my being.

234

Life is a lake of clear blue water.
It is our love that keeps us afloat.

235

As we grow with love,
Our branches reach out,
And our roots grow deeper and stronger.

236

I could not see the snow that was falling in the dark of the night,
But I could feel its purity and beauty.
Such as it is with the nature of our love.

237

The birds are quiet today,
But I can feel their love song.
I can feel your words of love in times of silence.

238

There is warmth from within that knows,
Our love will never feel the cold.

239

I asked nothing of your love.
Your light has joined mine.
We are a beacon of love.

240

Our love is not about the pot of gold.
Our love is about the rainbow itself.

241

There is a feeling of invitation that comes with our love,
We invite the universe to our coming out party.

242

We could easily be an island in an ocean of love.

243

Our love is more than we can humanly imagine.

244

Your love has been received.
It cannot be taken away.
You are now a part of me,
For all of eternity.

245

We are never alone.
We are a part of the light,
Cast by all those in the world that knows love.

246

We were attracted to each other's love.
Love will not rest,
Until everyone finds their love.

247

Fly high or low,
Fast or slow,
We are content to watch our love flow.

248

I am looking at your love,
And you are looking at mine.
We will soon see what our love story will be.

249

I once saw how I was different.
Then I saw your love.

250

1+1=1

251

Some doors opened and other doors closed,
As we walked the halls of our mansion of love.

252

It is so humbling to read my words about love.
There is more there than I thought possible.
I was just a dreamer without your love.

253

Our love challenges any sense of control,
I once thought I had to have.
Reason and caution have had their season.

254

I am helpless yet so alive,
Vulnerable yet willing to risk,
Ambitious yet at ease,
Now that I know the marvels of our love.

255

This moment of knowing your love,
Has lost its past.
It just wants to be true to thee.

256

Our love is expressed in endless days and endless ways.
The world turns and the winds blow.
While love is the magic carpet we ride on.

257

We play the game of life together,
We play the game with love.
The score is always 1 to 1.

258

We are on our journey through life.
It is our love that makes all things clear.

259

Our love is shared in many ways,
And communicated most deeply in the silence.

260

I am no different than thee.
We are a seed that became a tree.
Our roots touch with love.
Our leaves feel the same sun.
Our love is there for all to hang their swing on.

261

Shadows come and go but our love stays the same.
Things around us change but our love is still there.
We make many choices,
Knowing that we have already chosen each other.

262

Finding your love was easy,
Once the need was gone.

263

Our love is like the stars.
There is always one more to admire.
I look upon our love with awe and inspiration.
Our love is there when it cannot be seen.

264

The chair your love sits in is sometimes empty.
It is your chair and it has one purpose,
I am always ready for your love.

265

There was nothing to make right,
When we found each other's love.

266

New experiences flow by and we grow.
It is us that changes and not our love.

267

My eyes see differently now that I know love.
Now that I know love, I can see you.
Now that I see you,
I see the world with a new set of eyes.

268

Love, sweet love,
We will be as love was meant to be.
We will set you free for others to see.

269

Love, sweet love,
Have I found you or did you find me?

270

I closed my eyes and felt the love of everything around me,
I opened my eyes and saw your love.

271

Our acts of compassion and generosity have set us free to love.

272

The tree tops find their place in the sun to live.
We no longer reach for love.
Ours is a love found.

273

The flower being picked is saying thank you.
A flower standing in the field is there for everyone to see.
The flower on my table is love found.
It does matter where you are,
I know you have a place for me.

274

There is an excitement that comes with our love.
We cannot wait to experience the day that is before us.
It does not matter what it will bring.
It is our date with love.

275

There was a time when I tried to shed my innocence.
Your love has shown me,
That it is my innocence that has set me free.

276

Love leads to the discovery of worlds beyond our imagination.
Have we done everything we can to make this possible?

277

For all that I have I am grateful,
It is nothing to me without your love.
It is your love that makes this life all that it is.

278

It is love that makes our delicious what it is.

279

There is a growing certainty that our love will just be.
I let our love be what it will be as it grows with me.

280

While you are on my mind,
It is the grace of your love that I feel.

281

The words, "I love you," may warm your heart,
It is our words of love,
That gives life to this relationship.

282

When we do not know where our love is taking us,
We are not lost.

283

I see your love so much more clearly!
I know you feel the same.
It is not love that has changed,
It is love that has changed us.

284

Love is in the marvels of nature,
And we did not see all that we could have.
Love was in so many relationships,
And we did not see all that we should have.
Love is not a new way of seeing things,
Our love has made us so much more aware.
Greetings!

285

When I feel your love,
I love to feel.

286

Once upon a time,
It was easier to love,
Than it was to let someone love me.

287

Our love is always there.
We have set a course that is traveled with love.
Our future anticipates our love's arrival.

288

Love is my heaven.
You are my heavenly delight.

289

Love is the light that shines in the dark moments.
We are a light house signaling to the other.
The coast is clear; come this way!

290

Time flies by while our love stays young.
The details of experiences fade.
While it is the love that we remember.

291

I hear your love in the rustle of the leaves.
I feel your love under my feet.
We take our love for a walk every day.

292

I feel the comfort of your words,
While your love is doing the work.

293

You have introduced me to your love.
My mind is at peace to trust and dream.
Wants are few and far between.
My heart is full and my spirit is content.

294

We share a blanket as we sit on the beach of love.

295

We are like natures love.
We heal, nurture and inspire.
Our love is always there.

296

We live in a world of love so much bigger than us.
We are a grain of sand on a desert dune of love.

297

All conditions have dissolved in the presence of our love.
There is so much more for this love see.

298

This love is not a holiday feast,
It will not be enjoyed only to be hungry again.

299

Your love has washed my window.
Every day experiences seem more acute.
I am seeing life through a freshly polished looking glass.

300

Our time together on this earth will not be forever,
But it is recorded in our book of life as our love for each
other.

301

The grace of our love is not the end but the way.
We are in each other's heaven at the moment.

302

As this love is,
We know the nature of God.

303

Our love is a journey that brings with it,
The opportunity to sit among the flowers.

304

We dream because we love.
Every vision has you in it.

305

Love is our kingdom.
My love is your servant.
Your love is my fortune.

306

The love that inspires us,
Will take us beyond our dreams.

307

While it is your journey, let it be our love.
While it is my journey, let it be our love.
While it is our journey, let it be God's love.

308

There is no feast without love.

309

We see love in all that we have.

310

Love is the horse that pulls our cart.
One is not complete without the other.

311

This moment together is just a portion,
Of our infinite and eternal whole.

312

Love is our prayer.

313

Our daily bread is our love set free.

314

Before we were, we were love.
We are now two in love.
We are love found.

315

The lake has so many alcoves to explore.
There are many different reflections in the lake's mirror.
Our love is the lake itself.

316

Today, we stand amongst many as one love.
Tonight we rest under a blanket of gratitude.

317

Our love is as dependable as the blue that surrounds the cloud.

318

We are the body that houses the spirit of love.
We are a couple that brings love to life.

319

You are with me throughout the day.
Your love has been my companion.

320

The question has been answered.
There is enough for all.

321

Love opened the door that introduced us to our passion for life!
My passion for life has led me to your door step.

322

We wish that our love is felt by the powers that guide us.
We are asking that this love be felt by the rest of the world.

323

I am amazed at how meek I feel,
When I am in the presence of your love.

324

Our love is a journey and not a possession.
We can stand tall and walk straight.

325

We set in place an altar to honor our God.
We live a life that honors our love.

326

Perhaps I felt this love in my soul,
Well before my eyes and ears met you.

327

Our love is an awakening of two spirits.
There is nothing to hold us back.
Our joy comes from what we are able to share.

328

In the process of loving each other and ourselves,
We have shucked many oysters to find each other's pearl.

329

My journey with love brought me to this moment with you.

330

We affirm that we are who we were meant to be.

331

Our appreciation is our flower's seed of love.
Our garden grows for all to see.
Someday our neighbor's garden will touch ours.

332

We have a lot of fun exploring the boundaries of our
relationship.
The love came easy and the smiles are natural.
We leave the relationship alone to see what love will do next.

333

We give thanks for this wedding feast that nurtures our
bodies.
We give thanks for these bodies that express our love.
We give thanks for a creation that is able to feel that love.

334

Our love was brought into this heavenly relationship.
The two will never be separated.

335

This love flows through all that we do together.
Our expressions of love cannot be confined.

336

The light of our love is on and the table is always set.

337

Our love is as solid as the stone that anchors the mountain.

338

Our love is more than intellect can comprehend.

339

I have learned how to laugh at myself because of our love.
We laugh at a lot of things these days.

340

All life starts with the seed of perfection.
The seed knows what it will grow up to be.
Our times together nurture our seed of love.

341

Our love has unlimited potential.
The source of our love is endless.
Our time together is precious.

342

Trust anchors our love in place,
While faith takes our love to its greatest depth.

343

We walk a path together with a kind heart.
We see everyone as a precious being.
Our joy comes from savoring every moment of love.

344

If love was to play, it would swing with you.
If love was to smile, it would walk with you.
If love needed a place to stay, it would knock on your door.

345

Our love is a melody that keeps playing in my head.
Over and over,
I can't shut it off.

346

Our love knows how to find its way home.

347

Your love is the sweet rain that washes the path we walk on.

348

You are my love song.
Your love is music to my ears.

349

Our love for each other only begins with the poem.

350

We love each other,
As much as we love, love itself.

351

If love was to dream,
It would dream of you.

352

Our love is opening to the delicacies of our individuality.

353

The playfulness in our love is not about winning or losing.

354

We love for the delight of seeing each other's joy and happiness.

355

All is put at rest with you on my mind.

356

The sun always rises to greet our love.

357

Your garden of love is the endless nurture of its own beauty.
May I take a flower from your garden with me?

358

We are no longer courting.
Our love is the enchantment of this day.

359

This love is a dream that found its cloud to float on.

360

Accept my gratitude as my love in return.

361

It is love that makes all that we have worthwhile.

362

We appreciate the love everything along the way has provided.
Everyone has touched us with love.
Let this be the legacy of our love.

363

There are worlds unknown to us,
That will meet our love someday.

364

There would be no trip to take without our love.

365

Our love is under our feet and not on our shoulders.

Affirmations

Affirmations are a wonderful addition to our daily activities. You can feel the effect that an affirmation of love has upon you instantly. You will also find that an affirmation of love is an invaluable complement to any other personal affirmation. Affirmations of love work well because there is something within us that understands and feels words of love without any convincing needed. The intent of an affirmation is to replace a less desirable feeling with a feeling that is more desirable. Positive beliefs and the feelings that go with them lead to positive outcomes. The strength behind a belief is the emotional hold it has upon us. Love helps this process along because love carries its own intensity and believability.

A loving relationship is a beauty onto itself. The love of yourself and the life you live is a gift to any relationship. An affirmation of love gives you the feelings you need to face any of life's challenges together. Your feeling of love is the foundation of grace and serenity that a strong relationship is built upon. Be the love of all things around you so you can be the light that guides your relationships. An affirmation of love takes mystery to majesty in all relationships.

1. I feel free when I love.
2. My love is as vast as the cosmos.
3. I can find a guiding light in love.
4. I have the music of love within me.
5. Love puts a spring in my step.
6. I dance to the music of love.
7. My love flows around curves like a lazy river.
8. Love is a gift that creates.
9. I am protected by love.
10. My faith is my mansion of love.
11. My love flows with a harmonious ease.
12. World peace starts at home with my love.
13. My abundance was once a seed of love.
14. My sun rises and sets on love.
15. Patience is preceded by love.
16. I choose to set my words of love free.
17. I can feel the power of love at any time.
18. Love is as light as a feather dancing in a summer breeze.
19. Love keeps showing up in my tomorrow.
20. Now is my time for love.
21. Love is my vision and my state of being.
22. Love has a wisdom all its own.

23. Even a little bit of love has the light of the sun.

24. There is nothing I can do to master love. It is mine to set free.

25. I do not have to let love in, just let it out.

26. I am entitled to love.

27. The love I give is also a gift onto myself.

28. My love is simple and pure.

29. I was created to know love.

30. The love I breathe in, I breathe out.

31. I am the embodiment of love.

32. I let go of the past, replacing it with love.

33. I see love wherever I look.

34. I know love within myself.

35. No sacrifice is needed to find love.

36. Nothing can regulate my love.

37. I am free so that love can be.

38. My spirit is love.

39. I tune into the feelings of love with ease.

40. There is no fear where there is love.

41. I accept all that is given to me as love.

42. I include love in all perceptions.

43. I find love in my silence.

44. Love is my only goal this day.

45. Love is everywhere and in everything.

46. Love is my purpose.

47. Love gives me a new world to look at.

48. I choose to spend this day in perfect peace.

49. My love is now and forever.

50. Love is my being.

51. Love is my refuge and security.

52. I see only love with these eyes and ears.

53. Love is all around me.

54. The love I breathe in, I breathe out.

55. The peace of love is in my stillness.

56. If I am not free, love cannot be.

57. My love cannot be regulated.

58. My love stands on its own.

59. My love is more than this thought.

60. My love is the breath I take.

61. I feel my love with every one of my senses.

62. My love is simple and pure.

63. I can look within because I love.

64. My gratitude today is my path to love.

65. I accept all that is given to me this day as love.

66. The love I give to one, I give to all.

67. All I need to do is think of love and it is there.

68. Love is greater than all my parts.

69. We are joined together because of love.

70. My love is eternal.

71. No sacrifice is needed to find love.

72. The love I give is also a gift onto me.

73. Today I remember love, the rest is forgotten.

74. My love is felt wherever I go.
75. Love is part of my beauty.
76. All are one where there is love.
77. My gratitude and love go hand in hand.
78. I learn something new about love every day.
79. Love has healing powers.
80. Love has its own language.
81. Love gives me a light heart.
82. My laughter comes easy where there is love.
83. Love is my life force.
84. Love has a way of setting me free.
85. It is my delight to see the love in others.
86. My love is not an emotion. My love is a feeling that goes with knowing.
87. I know everything will be all right, I feel love.
88. My words might be comforting but it is love that is doing the work.
89. I do it with love.
90. I am the spirit of love.
91. I am as love is.
92. This is the moment of love.
93. Say yes to love.
94. I see love.
95. I see with love.
96. I feel with love.
97. My love flows.

98. We are one love.

99. Love is my heaven.

100. Love set me free.

101. I love.

102. Love is much bigger than even I can comprehend.

Author's Note

Words of love bring us comfort and offer us a feeling of hope. Words of love inspire us to dream and free us from hurt feelings. There is a lot of love within each of us that is looking for ways to be set free. The words presented in these writings are designed to stimulate the flow of your love feelings in order to enhance your expressions of love.

There are many marvels about love that we take for granted or simply overlook. The previous book to this one, "With Love as Love is", explains all of this in detail. That book also shows you how to heal from the past with the help of love. The book also shows you how to use the powers of love to bring happiness into all aspects of your life.

Visit the website: **withlovebygbradley.com** to view motivational messages regarding love. Use this site to share your thoughts and experiences regarding love with others. Share an original quote or verse about love and hopefully we will have a collection worthy of another publication. We can contribute the proceeds from that book to world charities and keep the flow of love strong.

Stay safe,
"Remember Who Loves You"
G. Bradley

Printed in the United States
By Bookmasters